EDUCATION LIBRARY SERVICE

Tel: 01606 275801

KT-405-391

BUILT FOR SUCCESS

THE STORY OF

Facebook

First published in the UK in 2013 by
Franklin Watts
338 Euston Road
London NW1 3BH

Franklin Watts Australia
Level 17/207 Kent Street
Sydney, NSW 2000

First published by Creative Education,
an imprint of The Creative Company.
www.thecreativecompany.us

Copyright © 2013 Creative Education.
International copyright reserved in all countries.
No part of this book may be reproduced in any
form without written permission from the publisher.

All rights reserved.

A CIP catalogue record for this book is available from the
British Library.

ISBN: 978 1 4451 2096 6

Dewey number: 338.7'61006754

Printed in China

Franklin Watts is a division of
Hachette Children's Books,
an Hachette UK company.

www.hachette.co.uk

DESIGN BY **ZENO DESIGN**
ART DIRECTION BY **RITA MARSHALL**

PHOTOGRAPHS BY Alamy (Art Directors & TRIP, CJG-Technology,
digitallife, NetPhotos, NetPics), Corbis (Rick Friedman, PHIL
McCARTEN/Reuters, BRIAN SNYDER/Reuters, Wu Kaixiang/
XinHua/Xinhua Press), Getty Images (Antoine Antoniol/
Bloomberg , Juana Arias/The Washington Post, Tony Avelar/
Bloomberg, Noah Berger/Bloomberg, Andrew Harrer/
Bloomberg, Gilles Mingasson, Leon Neal/AFP, Justin Sullivan,
Kimberly White)

Facebook® and the products discussed in this book are
either trademarks or registered trademarks of Facebook, Inc.
Trademarks associated with products of other companies
mentioned are the trademarks of their respective owners. This
is not an official publication of Facebook, Inc., and the views
set out herein are solely those of the author.

BUILT FOR SUCCESS

THE STORY OF

Facebook

W
FRANKLIN WATTS
LONDON • SYDNEY

SARA GILBERT

EDUCATION LIBRARY SERVICE 01606 275801	
RL	20-Aug-2013
	£ 13.99

On the afternoon of 4 February 2004, Mark Zuckerberg sat down at his desk in the accommodation he shared with three other Harvard University students. A few weeks earlier, the 19-year-old student had registered the **domain name** for a new website. He had spent his entire winter holiday hunched over his computer in his hall of residence, designing an online **social network** for fellow students. Now he was finally ready to launch the new site. As his computer hummed to life amidst the empty energy drinks cans and crumpled food packets, Zuckerberg prepared to click the final button that would make Thefacebook.com live – and which would start a web of connections that quickly criss-crossed the campus, the country and then the globe.

CHAPTER ONE

University connections

Mark Zuckerberg arrived at Harvard University in 2002 with a reputation as a computer whiz. He had been writing code since he was about 10 years old, when he developed games to play on his parents' home computer.

In high school [secondary school], Mark worked with a friend to create a **software** program that personalised music playlists according to a listener's preferences. Microsoft had reportedly offered almost £630,000 for the technology – and Zuckerberg and his friend had turned it down, a fact that was well known among students at Harvard's Cambridge, Massachusetts campus in the USA.

Zuckerberg, who studied computer science, wasn't interested in programming to get rich. It was a hobby, something that came naturally to the gifted adolescent, and that attracted attention on campus. Students appreciated the Course Match site he developed as a second-year student, as it allowed them to select their classes based on other students already enrolled so that they could be with friends. The Facemash site he created that same year, however, was not so widely adored. The site placed photos of Harvard students side by side and asked viewers to rank them according to looks. After launching Facemash, Zuckerberg was summoned before the university's administrative board and put

on **probation** (an American university alternative to suspension) for **hacking** into the university's systems to obtain the photos.

Not long after the Facemash controversy, Zuckerberg became consumed by another programming project: an online social network that would allow Harvard students to connect with each other. Although his motives were primarily social, Zuckerberg recognised that this new website had the potential to become a business that might eventually generate a little income as well. To help him stay on top of the business, Zuckerberg became partners with business student Eduardo Saverin, who matched Zuckerberg's investment of £630 ($1,000) to pay for the **servers** needed to host the site, and also gave financial advice.

Zuckerberg called the site 'Thefacebook.com', after the online photo collections for each hall of residence at Harvard, which the students called 'facebooks'. The only requirement for registration on the site was an active Harvard email address. Users created profile pages that included a photo and personal information – whether they were single or in a relationship, for example, as well as lists of their favourite books, films, musical groups and more. Each user could invite other students to be their 'friends' on Thefacebook, and could limit who would be able to view the information they posted on their page.

Almost as soon as Thefacebook went live on 4 February 2004, several dozen students who heard about it from friends signed up. Four days later, more than 650 students were using the site. Thefacebook became one of the hottest topics around campus. Within three weeks, it had 6,000 users – including undergraduate and graduate students, **alumni**, faculty and staff.

The task of working out the glitches of Thefacebook's design and keeping its rapid growth from crashing the servers quickly became overwhelming. Zuckerberg hired one of his roommates, Dustin Moskovitz, to help him keep up. Although Zuckerberg couldn't pay Moskovitz in cash, he promised him a 5 per cent ownership stake in the site. As the creator, Zuckerberg held 65 per cent and Saverin held 30 per cent.

Eight days younger than Zuckerberg, Dustin Moskovitz (shown here) helped design the Facebook site

While Zuckerberg's time was spent tweaking Thefacebook's code and making it run smoothly, Moskovitz's role was handling requests from students at other American universities wanting access to Thefacebook. The site went live at Columbia University on 25 February; it was launched at Stanford University the next day and Yale University three days later, connecting students at the various universities with one another. The immediate popularity of this social network prompted a reporter from the *Stanford Daily* to interview Zuckerberg about his intentions with Thefacebook.com. "I know it sounds corny," he said. "But I'd love to improve people's lives, especially socially."

When calls from journalists began coming more often, Zuckerberg recruited his more articulate roommate, Chris Hughes, to serve as Thefacebook's official spokesperson. Hughes reiterated a point Zuckerberg made often: the goal was not to make money, but to provide a fun, worthwhile service to students.

But as Thefacebook spread from campus to campus and registered users grew to more than 30,000 by the end of March 2004, Zuckerberg realised that he would have to find some source of **revenue** to offset the ballooning costs of running the business. Thefacebook was paying £285 ($450) a month for the five servers it required to stay up and running, and more servers would certainly be needed in the near future. Saverin started selling a few advertisements that began appearing on Thefacebook in April, and invested another £6,300 ($10,000) in the company. Zuckerberg, meanwhile, fielded calls from people who wanted to invest in the site – including an offer to purchase the four-month-old business for £6.3 million ($10 million).

Zuckerberg wasn't interested. In six months, Thefacebook had spread to 34 campuses and had accumulated 100,000 users. He was so committed to the site and its growth that he decided to move to northern California's Silicon Valley, a longtime hotbed for technology **start-ups**, over the summer. "[It] was kind of this mythical place where all the techs used to come from," he told a journalist. "So I was like, I want to check that out."

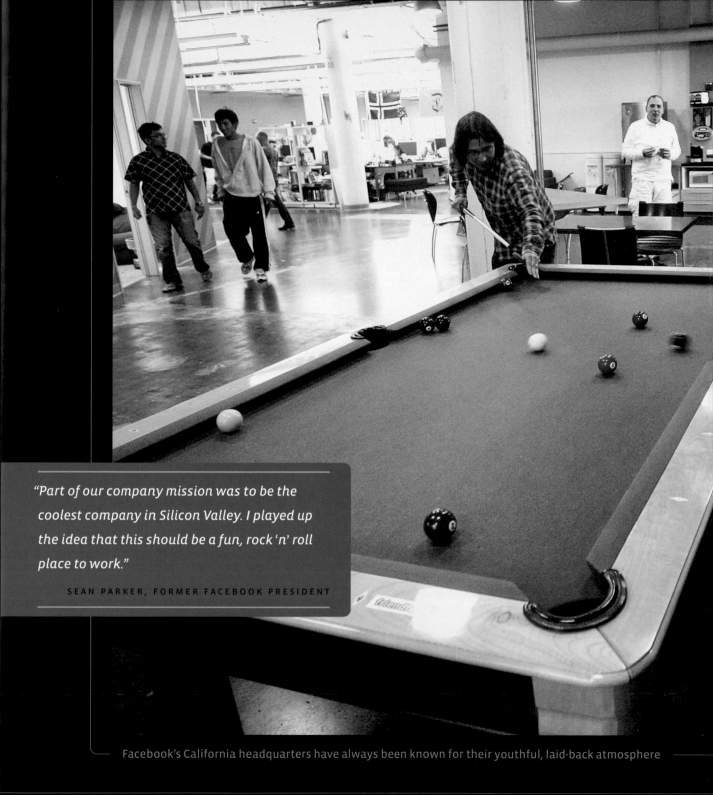

> "Part of our company mission was to be the coolest company in Silicon Valley. I played up the idea that this should be a fun, rock 'n' roll place to work."
>
> SEAN PARKER, FORMER FACEBOOK PRESIDENT

Facebook's California headquarters have always been known for their youthful, laid-back atmosphere

FROM FRIENDSTER
TO FACEBOOK

Although Facebook has become the world's most widely used social networking site it certainly wasn't the first. Almost 10 years before Mark Zuckerberg launched Thefacebook in 2004, Match.com started helping people find dates, while Classmates.com started helping people connect with former school friends in 1995. Although neither of these sites was much like modern social networks they initiated the idea that people could connect with each other online. In 1997, a site called Sixdegrees.com took the idea further, attempting to build a network based on shared relationships amongst users. But it was the social networking site Friendster, launched in 2003, that caught Zuckerberg's attention – and that focused his mission for Facebook. One of the lessons he learnt from Friendster was to invest adequately in servers to keep the site running. Friendster had notoriously slow servers that often crashed, which led to its ultimate demise.

CHAPTER TWO

Five million friends

Zuckerberg, Moskovitz and two **interns** rented a house in Palo Alto, California for the summer of 2004. They had no car and very little furniture. Their dining room table was piled high with computers, modems and cameras, as well as empty bottles and drinks cans. Like many university students, they avoided early mornings. Often they'd start working in the afternoon and keep at it until well after midnight.

They had another collaborator working with them as well: Sean Parker, who had been involved with the online music sharing service, Napster, as well as other Internet ventures. Parker admired the concept behind Thefacebook and immediately liked Zuckerberg, whom he had met at a dinner in New York earlier that year. Although Parker had yet to turn 25 years old, he became the oldest and most experienced member of Thefacebook's team when he joined the operation during the summer of 2004.

Zuckerberg, Moskovitz and the interns spent their time improving Thefacebook .com, bolstering its servers and writing computer code for new features and services, including ways for users to send private messages to each other. Parker, meanwhile, devoted much of his time to helping Thefacebook become a

Like Zuckerberg, Sean Parker (shown here) was a computer prodigy, having begun programming aged six bona fide business. He had become acquainted with a network of potential investors during his time with other Internet companies, and approached them again for Thefacebook.

Zuckerberg still wasn't sure that he wanted to invite investors into the business, and didn't want to rely too heavily on advertising, either. But Thefacebook was going to need more funds than the tiny amount trickling in from advertisers. Zuckerberg had already spent almost £12,600 ($20,000) on new equipment, primarily servers. "I need servers just as much as I need food," Zuckerberg said that summer. "I could probably go a while without eating, but if we don't have enough servers then the site is screwed."

By the end of the summer, the site's 200,000 users were straining the company's **infrastructure**. So in the autumn of 2004, Parker arranged a meeting with Peter Thiel, co-founder of the secure online payment system known as PayPal, who was now privately investing in Internet start-ups. Even though Zuckerberg wore a T-shirt, jeans and flip-flops – his usual outfit – to the meeting, Thiel was impressed by both the young chief executive officer (CEO) and Thefacebook site. He offered a loan of £315,000, which would eventually give him a 10 per cent stake in the company. A handful of other private investors contributed another £63,000 ($100,000) to the company's resources.

This infusion of cash convinced Zuckerberg and Moskovitz not to return to Harvard in the autumn. Instead, they moved into an office above a Chinese restaurant on Emerson Street in Palo Alto, hired artists to paint colourful murals on the walls, and bought cheap furniture that they had to put together themselves. They also introduced a pair of new features for users. The first was a 'wall' where friends could post comments and notes. The second was the Groups function, which allowed users to unite around any common bond, from courses they were taking to drinks they enjoyed. Membership grew to 400,000 in September and then to 500,000 in October. The one-millionth user registered on 30 November.

From its earliest days, Facebook invited user suggestions, as on this scribble board in Palo Alto

In the face of such rapid growth, Zuckerberg and his team realised that the £378,000 they had received from investors wasn't going to last very long. Private investors and venture capital firms (which give large sums of money to new and emerging companies in exchange for an ownership stake) began ringing Zuckerberg. He was surprised when one company offered to buy Thefacebook outright for £47 million. But after months of evaluating competing offers, in May 2005 Zuckerberg accepted £8 million from the venture capital company Accel Partners. In return, Accel Partners received 15 per cent ownership of the company, which officially became known simply as Facebook a few months later.

The new investment meant that Zuckerberg could upgrade his growing network of servers. It also meant that he could start hiring more people to help build and maintain the site. He planted a wooden menu board on the pavement in front of the office block, with positions such as director of **engineering** advertised in chalk. Eventually, Facebook also hired a recruiter to find and hire software engineers so that Zuckerberg could focus his own efforts on the wider needs of Facebook.

One of the issues on his mind was expanding Facebook. By autumn 2005, the site was operating at more than 1,800 colleges and universities. At least 85 per cent of the university students in America were registered users and more than half of them visited the site daily. Zuckerberg was eager to reach new **demographics**, and believed that high school students were a natural next step.

In September, Facebook officially invited high school students to register on the site – but there was a catch. Because few schools issue email addresses to all students, as most universities do, Facebook couldn't verify the identities of individuals. The solution was for registered university users to invite their younger friends to join Facebook; those new members could then invite their friends and so on. By the following spring, more than 1 million of the 5.5 million active 'Facebookers' were high school students.

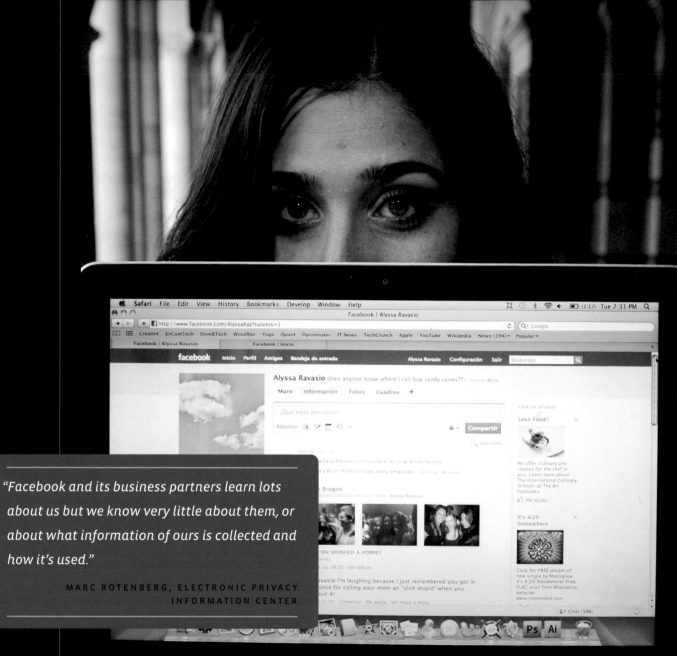

"Facebook and its business partners learn lots about us but we know very little about them, or about what information of ours is collected and how it's used."

MARC ROTENBERG, ELECTRONIC PRIVACY INFORMATION CENTER

MacBook Pro

Facebook competed with – and eventually trounced – another social networking site called Myspace

Cameron (left) and Tyler Winklevoss

LEGAL WRANGLING

Before Facebook had been around a whole year, its founder was hit with a lawsuit related to the site. It came from three fellow Harvard students who, in 2003, had asked for Zuckerberg's help designing a dating and socialising website they planned to call Harvard Connection. Zuckerberg agreed to join the crew, but later bowed out, saying he was too busy to carry on working. When Facebook launched shortly after, the students – twins Cameron and Tyler Winklevoss and Divya Narendra – claimed Zuckerberg had stolen their idea, and decided to challenge him in court. Zuckerberg shrugged it off, saying the sites were "completely different" and calling their threats "ridiculous". He hired lawyers to fight the charges, including copyright **infringement**, and settled the suit with a £12.7 million cash payment and Facebook **stock** to Narendra and the Winklevoss brothers in 2008. Although they accepted the settlement, the Winklevoss brothers attempted to reopen the case in 2010.

CHAPTER THREE

Growing pains

A mere two years into its existence, Facebook was undeniably successful, not only in America and Canada, but also in the United Kingdom, where the service was now available. The photo **application** it had launched in late 2005, which allowed users to post photos to the site and share them with friends, had been a huge hit. But Facebook was still burning through millions of dollars just to maintain its servers and upgrade its technology.

Although suitors continued to ring with offers to buy the company, Zuckerberg resisted. He did begin to think more seriously about allowing advertisements to be displayed alongside the information on a user's page, something he had opposed in the past. But if they could help fund continued expansion, he was now willing to consider small, well-placed ads that didn't distract from Facebook's content. Most of the early advertising was customised; companies created sponsored groups for certain products, and paid Facebook according to how many users signed up. Proctor & Gamble, for example, created a 'Smile State' group promoting Crest White Strips – and promised free film tickets to anyone who joined the group.

Facebook's photo application became hugely popular, allowing for quick and easy image sharing

More than 20,000 people did. Zuckerberg appreciated advertising that allowed companies to connect with customers without actually running banner ads on the pages – but he turned down £63,000 from Sprite to turn Facebook's home page green for a day to promote the soft drink.

Meanwhile, Facebook's engineers were planning to reach out to a new audience again. Zuckerberg had decided that workplaces, where most adult social interaction occurs, should be the next frontier, so in May 2006 Facebook launched work networks to connect adults with others in their workplaces. But to his surprise work networks flopped. Few, if any, people signed up, in part because there had been little advance **marketing**. Zuckerberg was crushed and a black cloud hung over the office. "It was the most wrong he'd ever been at Facebook, and the first time he'd ever been wrong in a big way," said Matt Cohler, one of Zuckerberg's closest advisers in the company.

That disappointment was muted by the August announcement of a strategic relationship with software maker Microsoft to develop and sell banner ads for the site, which Zuckerberg had agreed to accept. That partnership opened up a lucrative advertising stream that immediately turned 2006 into the company's first **profitable** year. With his confidence restored, Zuckerberg prepared to launch two of the company's biggest initiatives in September 2006.

The first was News Feed, which would collect the most recent and relevant information about each user's friends and create a scrolling News Feed screen for the user to view. When a friend uploaded new photos, changed a piece of information, or updated his or her status, it would appear on the News Feed screen. It was a complex project that had the potential to revolutionise the way users interacted. No longer would they have to click on their friends' pages to see what they were doing; News Feed brought the information to them.

The second project was another attempt to broaden Facebook's audience. Zuckerberg remained convinced that Facebook could be a tool for people of all ages to connect with friends, and had decided that 'open registration'

Search

Search · 0 searches >> 0 Ne

OK · Safe Web ▾ · 🔒 Identity Saf

r search activity - your images · ☒ · 🔳 f **Fa**

Search

📋 News Feed

Share: · 📄 **Status** · 🖼 Photo · 🔗 Link

omg did you see that friday

– which would make the site available to anyone, anywhere – would begin in the autumn. As one team of engineers worked day and night preparing for the launch of News Feed, another team created a service to help open-registration users find friends based on names in their email address books.

News Feed launched early in the morning on 5 September. But as the Facebook team swigged champagne directly from the bottle in celebration, users started complaining in Facebook posts and emails that the new format was an invasion of their privacy. They begged for it to be turned off. One user created a group called 'Students Against Facebook News Feed', which had more than 100,000 members within 24 hours.

The staff was astounded. The information available through News Feed had previously been available to users' friends anyway. News Feed just made access to updates easier and more immediate. But Zuckerberg remained remarkably calm. He saw the **viral** response to News Feed's release as evidence that it was effective, as users were taking advantage of the feature to spread their opinions about it. He knew, however, that the company had to respond. So he instituted new privacy features that would give users control over what information was posted on the News Feed. Then he sent a message to Facebook users: "We really messed this one up," he wrote, apologising for not better preparing them for the new features. He explained what the company was doing in response to their complaints. And just as quickly as it had started the anti-News Feed movement fizzled out.

Now the Facebook staff prepared for the 26 September beginning of open registration. But instead of sipping champagne immediately, they spent the first two weeks after the launch huddled anxiously over data about new users, looking for some indication of success. By early October they had it. New users were joining at a rate of 50,000 per day – a significant increase over the 20,000 per day prior to open registration, and an indication that older users were eagerly signing up for the service.

"I want everybody here to be careful about what you post on Facebook, because in the YouTube [Internet video] age whatever you do will be pulled up later somewhere in your life."

US PRESIDENT BARACK OBAMA

Politicians – including US president Barack Obama – came to recognise Facebook's growing influence

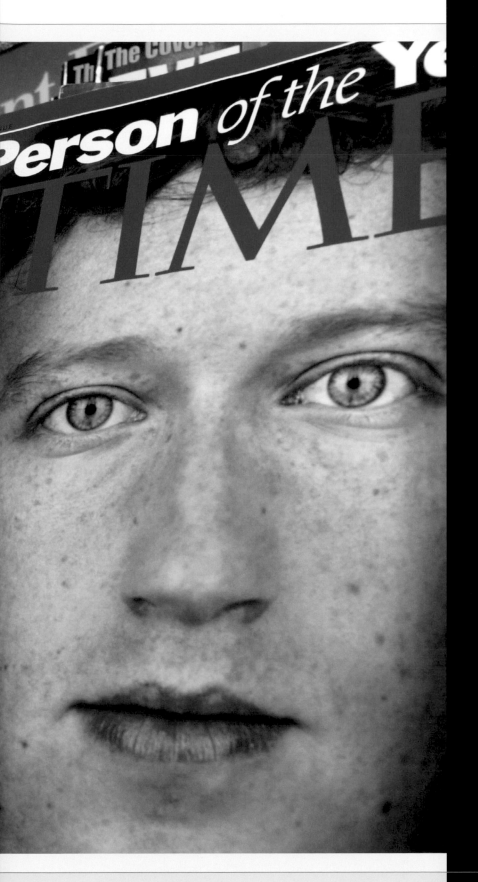

CELEBRITY STATUS

Mark Zuckerberg has garnered a reputation for being shy, soft-spoken and intensely private about his personal life – and the fame and notoriety he's earned as Facebook's founder hasn't changed him. Even after his company had made him a billionaire, Zuckerberg was most commonly seen wearing the shorts, hooded sweatshirt and flip-flop sandals that he had preferred as a university student. But his celebrity status came with a price. Zuckerberg became so recognisable that people often interrupted him at restaurants and other public places to ask for an autograph or a picture with him. Such intrusions became more common after a film about Facebook was released in 2010. *The Social Network* was one of the most popular films of the year, but Zuckerberg was not amongst its fans. "I started Facebook to improve the world and make it a more transparent place – and this movie portrays me as someone who built Facebook so I could meet girls," he said.

CHAPTER FOUR

More than friends

The 22-year-old Zuckerberg transported all 150 Facebook employees to California's Great America theme park in Santa Clara for a holiday party at the end of 2006. But when they returned to the company's offices, which were now scattered throughout several buildings located on Palo Alto's University Avenue, it was time to get serious about business.

Facebook was being used by more than 12 million people around the world, a number that grew by tens of thousands daily. But there was still plenty of additional work to be done.

Zuckerberg knew that Facebook's photo application wasn't perfect; the photos weren't high **resolution** and the printing function didn't work well. He also knew that a new event invitation function, which would allow users to notify their friends about upcoming activities in which they might be interested, was extremely basic. Even so, both photos and events were incredibly popular on Facebook – proof that users weren't looking for sophisticated software as much as functional connections with their friends.

Palo Alto, California has fewer than 70,000 people, but looms large as a hotspot for tech companies

This realisation helped push the next big idea for Facebook, one that Zuckerberg had been obsessing about since the company's earliest days: becoming a **platform** on which other software applications could be built and run. His roots as a programmer fuelled his desire to open the door for other aspiring engineers and software designers to create new applications for Facebook users. He assumed that the web of connections between those users would allow the best applications to spread rapidly throughout the network.

Zuckerberg was so excited about the idea that he hired an event planner to prepare a glitzy launch party. On the day of the party, more than 750 people – including journalists and representatives from software and Internet companies – packed into a hotel ballroom. "Together, we're starting a movement," Zuckerberg told the crowd. Then he demonstrated how the new Facebook platform could be used to create applications. Afterwards, he invited developers to join him for an eight-hour, hands-on software development session in which participants had the opportunity to begin working on actual applications (or apps, as they became known). The immediate reactions were overwhelmingly positive. Six months after the launch, more than 250,000 developers were operating 25,000 approved applications on Facebook, from the Graffiti app that let users 'scribble' notes on their friends' pages, to poker and word games. Zuckerberg particularly enjoyed a Scrabble-like game that helped him convince his grandparents to join Facebook and play it with him online.

Facebook Platform elevated the company's standing as a technology company, not just a media company. It gave many of its users a reason to visit more often and to stay on the site longer. And it helped turn many of the small developers who were contributing applications into prosperous businesses, as they were able to either charge for use of their apps or to sell advertising alongside them.

But Facebook, meanwhile, was again in need of more money. As the site grew to more than 50 million users in autumn 2007, half of whom lived outside

the USA, the challenge to build and maintain a suitable infrastructure grew as well. The first thought was to seek out new investors interested in owning a small stake in the company – and many were, thanks to the glow surrounding Facebook in light of its international growth and the success of its platform. Amongst those eager to invest were both Google and Microsoft, rival companies who also wanted to negotiate advertising rights for the site. In October, a deal with Microsoft was announced that surprised many observers because of its size. Microsoft invested £151 million ($240 million) in Facebook in exchange for 1.6 per cent of the company.

Facebook's financial outlook brightened again in November, when Zuckerberg announced Facebook Ads, an advertising system that he was more comfortable incorporating into the site. Businesses could build pages and seek Facebook 'fans'. Individuals signed up as fans of a particular company and, in turn, occasionally received special opportunities or timely information. The companies could also develop small adverts that could be targeted to appear on the pages of specific user groups, based on users' ages, locations and even products and services they had purchased. Facebook gathered all of that information through online tracking systems.

The use of such information, paired with a new Facebook application known as Beacon, became one of the company's worst blunders. Beacon inserted notes about purchases users made online into the News Feeds of friends. Not only did that feel like an invasion of privacy to many people, but it also spoilt surprises for others. A woman found out that she was getting a diamond ring for Christmas when a post on her Facebook News Feed noted that her husband had purchased one at Overstock.com.

Zuckerberg was surprised by the furor caused over Beacon. Once again, the Facebook CEO had to make a public apology about a problematic feature. "We simply did a bad job with this release," he finally admitted, as he announced that users could opt in or out of Beacon. "I apologise for it."

"Our mission since day one has been to make society more open... We help people be more open across more contexts."

DAVE MORIN, LONGTIME FACEBOOK EMPLOYEE

Although Facebook aspired to draw users of all ages, most of its users – and employees – were young

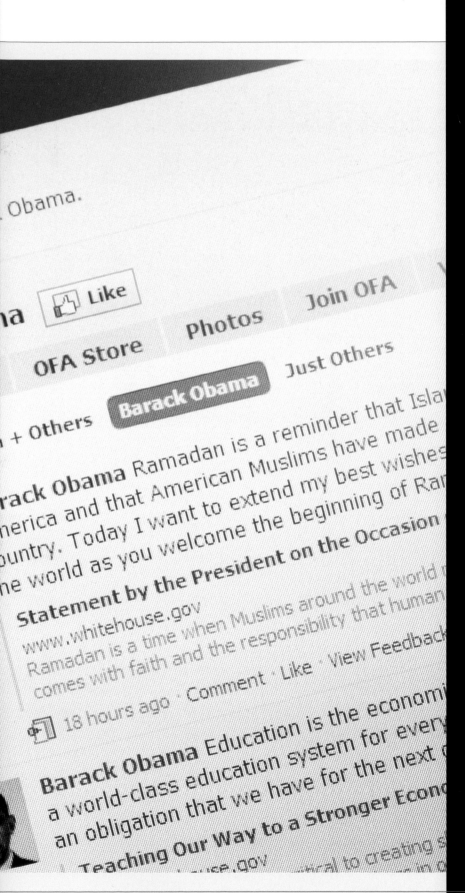

Obama.

Like

OFA Store   Photos   Join OFA

+ Others   Barack Obama   Just Others

rack Obama Ramadan is a reminder that Isla
merica and that American Muslims have made
untry. Today I want to extend my best wishes
ne world as you welcome the beginning of Ra

Statement by the President on the Occasion
www.whitehouse.gov
Ramadan is a time when Muslims around the world
comes with faith and the responsiblity that human

18 hours ago · Comment · Like · View Feedback

Barack Obama Education is the economi
a world-class education system for every
an obligation that we have for the next
Teaching Our Way to a Stronger Econo

POLITICALLY INVOLVED

From the beginning, some Facebook users proudly posted their political beliefs on the site. Eventually, the politicians they often wrote about began to create their own Facebook pages as well. In 2008, Facebook became a prominent venue for discussion among its members and the candidates running for office – including the two major US presidential candidates, senators John McCain and Barack Obama. Obama strategically hired Chris Hughes, one of the original Facebook founders, to help run the online component of his campaign for president. With Hughes's help, Obama created a strong following on Facebook, amassing more than a million friends during the course of the campaign. In the process, he extended his message to a younger audience that didn't always pay heed to traditional media outlets. The strategy worked; Obama received almost 70 per cent of the vote among Americans younger than 25 in what became known to many observers as 'the Facebook election'.

CHAPTER FIVE

Private matters

Although some users were still angry with Facebook, the company decided to move forward with its plans for growth. Early in 2008, it made sites available in Spanish, French and German for its European users. In April, it launched Facebook Chat, an instant messaging format that allowed friends who were on Facebook at the same time to type instant messages to each other.

In the midst of all this, the privacy concerns that had been stirred up by the Beacon release were simmering in the background. Users were growing more and more alarmed by the amount of information Facebook knew about them, and by who might have access to that information. In March, the company announced updated privacy controls that allowed users to decide how much of their information would be available to all Facebook users. They could also limit certain parts of their profiles to people who were registered as their friends or to anyone registered as a friend of one of their friends.

Although some within Facebook thought the controls should go further, Zuckerberg believed that people should be allowed and even encouraged to share

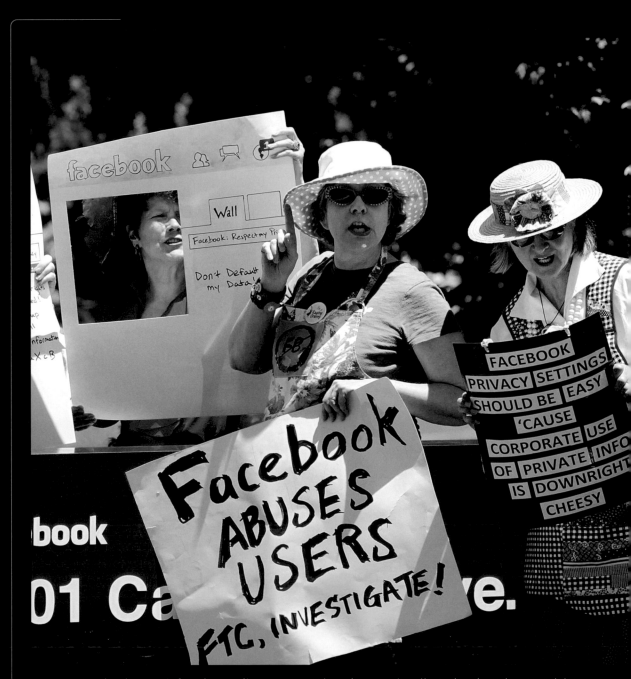

As Facebook grew, it faced sporadic protests against the ways it collected and used personal data

BUILT FOR SUCCESS

PAGE 40

information freely. He wrote frequently in **blog** posts that users should have a right to control their own information – but that he also envisaged a more open and transparent society in which more information would be public.

To that end Zuckerberg introduced a new set of privacy controls late in 2009, and instructed all Facebook users to adjust their settings again. The new feature this time was an 'everyone' option, which allowed users to select certain pieces of information they were willing to share with all of Facebook's 350 million users. In the process, however, Facebook made 'everyone' the **default** for all information pending each user's adjustment. This meant that many Facebook members who weren't paying attention, or who didn't take the time to check their privacy settings, were suddenly more exposed than they realised. Facebook also made all users' names, profile pictures and genders publicly available by default. And then there were the random glitches that occasionally sent private messages to unintended recipients or that made private chats public.

Users were again up in arms – but they weren't the only ones. In December 2009, a group of 10 privacy organisations jointly filed a formal complaint with the US Federal Trade Commission (FTC). They sought an investigation into Facebook's handling of information, and wished to levy financial penalties against the company. By early 2010, four US senators had joined the campaign as well, asking the FTC to set new privacy guidelines for Facebook and other social networking sites.

Despite his preference to be as open as possible, Zuckerberg had to address the complaints. He arranged meetings with privacy **advocates** and with New York senator Charles Schumer, one of the lawmakers who had called on the FTC to look into Facebook's practices. With their input, in May 2010, Facebook rolled out a redesigned privacy policy that simplified the choices and offered users more powerful controls over their own information. "When people have control over what they share, they want to share more," he explained.

THE STORY OF FACEBOOK

Search

Choose Your Privacy Settings

🗂 **Connecting on Facebook**
Control basic information your friends will use to find y

🔒 **Sharing on Facebook**
These settings control who can see what you share.

Everyone

Friends of Friends

Friends Only

Your stat

Bio and

Family

Photo

Relig

Birth

Facebook responded to user concerns by broadening the options for controlling the viewing of information

"When people share more, the world becomes more open and connected... The number one thing we've heard is that many users want a simpler way to control their information."

In early 2010, Facebook's membership numbered 400 million; by July that figure had grown to 500 million – more than the populations of America, Canada and Mexico combined. Zuckerberg had moved the company's employees to a big, trendy building in Palo Alto, where many of the walls and doors were giant white boards on which employees could scribble ideas and work out new plans. Breakfast was served to employees, who often rolled round the office on skateboards. The company's revenue was continuing to grow as well; in 2009, revenue was reportedly close to £441 million.

As a private company, Facebook wasn't required to release its financial information publicly. But by the end of 2010, many insiders, including Peter Thiel, one of Facebook's first investors, were predicting that the company would eventually become a publicly held business with **shares** traded on the stock market. Everyone knew the timing would be up to Zuckerberg, who remained the CEO of Facebook and who controlled the largest block of stock in the company as well. Indeed, in February 2012, Zuckerberg announced that Facebook would go public and sell stock later in the year.

Zuckerberg had always been reluctant to discuss his financial goals for the company because he maintained that the money didn't matter as much as the benefits Facebook provided. But he didn't shy away from defining his future objectives for Facebook: to reach billions of users and to provide the best possible service to them.

Those are the same objectives Zuckerberg had for his social networking website when he launched it in his hall of residence on a winter's day in 2004. Although he may not have envisaged it growing to hundreds of millions of users around the world on that day, his intent to create connections amongst people and forge a more open atmosphere was the same then as it is now.

"My goal was never just to create a company... [but to] build something that actually makes a big change in the world."

MARK ZUCKERBERG, FACEBOOK FOUNDER

By late 2011, Mark Zuckerberg was one of the world's richest people, with £8.5 billion

CAUGHT ON FACEBOOK

No matter how many privacy controls Facebook implemented, it couldn't stop people posting things that might get them into trouble. Parents, schools, employers and even law enforcement officers were all easily able to find incriminating evidence on the site. In one example a high school student in Massachusetts searched through Facebook looking for pictures of classmates drinking and sent them to the principal. Another high school principal scanned through Facebook himself, looking for pictures of athletes at parties – and he suspended those he found holding bottles of lager. But it wasn't just students getting into trouble: a young employee who told his boss he needed to take time off due to a family crisis was caught out when a friend posted a picture of him at a party on Facebook. And in New York, a police detective was demoted after posting a racially charged status update when Barack Obama was elected president.

GLOSSARY

advocates people or groups who support and defend a particular cause or interest

alumni a graduate or former student of a particular university

application a software program designed to help a user perform tasks, play games or take other action on a computer or computerised device

blog an online journal with regular written entries and comments from readers

default a pre-selected option adopted by a computer program when no other alternative is specified by the user

demographics certain segments of the population, identified by statistics such as age or income, usually for advertising purposes

domain name the words or symbols that serve as an address for a computer network or website

engineering a profession in which people design or build computer systems to solve problems

hacking gaining access to a computer, or information on a computer, without permission

infrastructure the underlying foundation and framework of an organisation or company, which includes its employees and leaders as well as buildings and equipment

infringement an encroachment on or limitation of the rights of another person

interns advanced students or graduates who work, with supervision, in a professional position to gain experience in a certain field

marketing the process of promoting products or services

platform the base from which new computer programs and applications can be built and operated

probation at American universities, a period of time during which a person's actions are closely monitored to ensure that no rules are broken

profitable making more money than is spent

resolution the degree of detail visible in a photographic, television or screen image

revenue the money earned by a company; another word for income

servers the main computers in a network, or group of linked computers, on which shared programs and files are stored

shares the equal parts a company may be divided into; shareholders each hold a certain number of shares, or a percentage, of the company

social network a group of people linked in an online setting by common ties, such as friendship, employment or other affiliations

software written programs or rules that control a computer's operations

start-ups companies that are in the early stages of operation

stock shared ownership in a company by many people who buy shares, or portions, of stock, hoping the company will make a profit and the stock value will increase

viral spreading from person to person rapidly, especially online

2003	Mark Zuckerberg creates Course Match and Facemash while at Harvard University
2004	Zuckerberg partners with Eduardo Saverin Thefacebook networking site up and running The company moves to California to expand
2005	Thefacebook becomes known as Facebook Zuckerberg accepts £8 million from Accel Partners for 15 per cent ownership Photo application launched
2006	Facebook is made available to all through open registration The News Feed is launced Google applications are created
2007	Over 50 million people use Facebook Microsoft invests £151 million into Facebook for 1.6 per cent ownerhsip
2008	Political parties begin using Facebook as a means to reach voters Site made available in Spanish, French and German Facebook Chat launched
2009-2010	Several organisations file complaints against Facebook regarding privacy and information sharing
2010	The film *The Social Network* is released Facebook users reach 500 million
2012	Facebook goes public and sells shares

INDEX